Basic Rules *

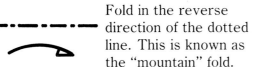 Fold in the reverse direction of the dotted line. This is known as the "mountain" fold.

Fold along the dotted line in the direction of the arrow. This is called the "valley" fold.

—— Cut

SAILBOAT Ⓐ

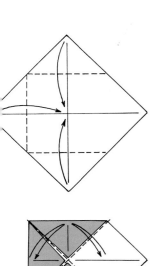

Make creases.

Make creases.

Make creases.

④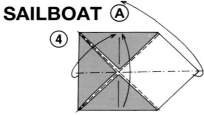

Fold following creases.

⑤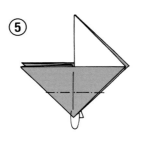

finished

SAILBOAT Ⓑ

④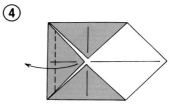

⑤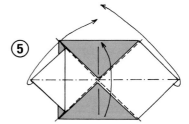

⑥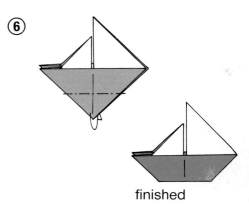

finished

CE-CREAM

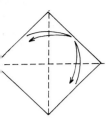

Make creases.

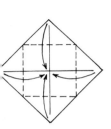

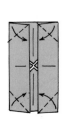

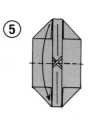
⑤

⑥

Fold outside corners toward inside.

⑦

CONE

①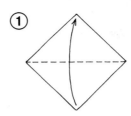

②

③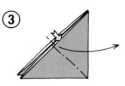

Put finger inside, lift and flatten.

④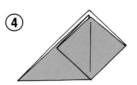

Do the same on the opposite side.

⑤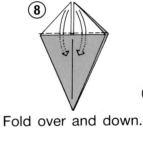

⑥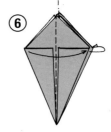

⑦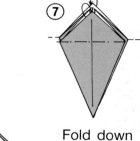

Fold down into inside.

⑧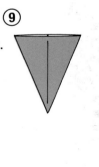

Fold over and down.

⑨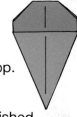

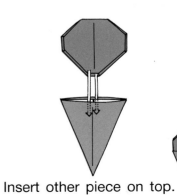

Insert other piece on top.

finished

4

HEN AND CHICK

CHICK

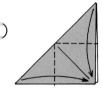

Make a crease.

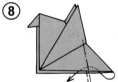

Turn it over.

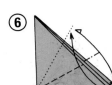
⑥

⑦ Fold down
toward inside.

⑧ Fold down
toward inside.

finished

HEN

①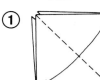
Begin with Step ⑤
for "CHICK", turned
upside down.

②
Put finger inside,
spread and flatten.

③
Do the same on
the opposite side.

④
Fold top layer back
and to the outside.

⑤ Fold toward inside.

⑥ Fold toward inside.

finished

6

JACKET

See page 13.

①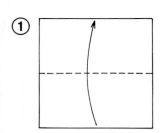

②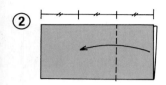

③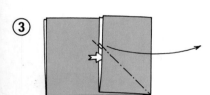

Put finger inside,
spread and flatten.

④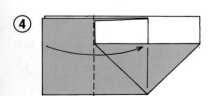

⑤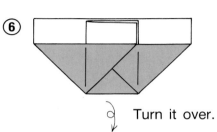

Put finger inside,
spread and flatten.

⑥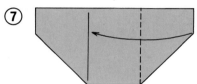

Turn it over.

⑦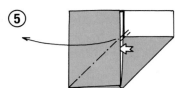

⑧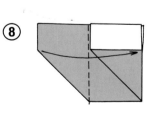

⑨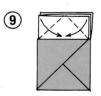

⑩

Return top
right flap
to top right corner.

⑪

Fold the top right flap
down and under.

⑫

Repeat Steps ⑨ – ⑪
on the opposite side.

finished

PURSE

①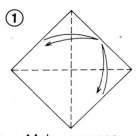

Make creases.

②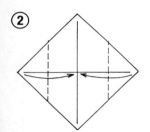

③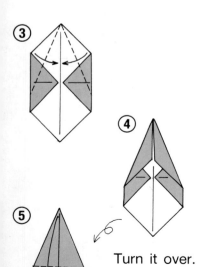

④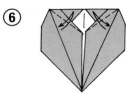

⑤

Turn it over.

⑥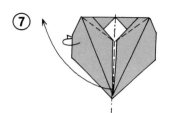

Make creases.

⑦

Pinch sides and pull up.

⑧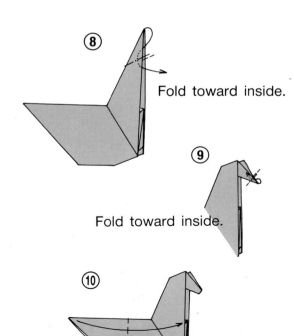

Fold toward inside.

⑨

Fold toward inside.

⑩

⑪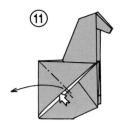

Put finger inside,
spread and flatten.

⑫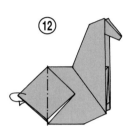

⑬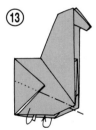

Fold outside layers in.

finished

11

HORSE

JACKET Ⓐ

① Make a crease.

②

③

④ Put finger inside, spread and flatten.

⑤

⑥

⑦

⑧ $\frac{1}{4}$

⑨

⑩ Turn it over.

⑪

⑫

Paste on buttons.

3623

Turn it over.　finished

JACKET Ⓑ

Start with Step ③ for "JACKET Ⓐ".

① Fold over a little less than one third.

②

③ Return to original position.

④ Put finger inside, spread and flatten.

⑤

⑥

⑦

⑧

⑨

⑩

⑪

Paste on botto

finished